Table of Content

Faith Creates New Incredible Patterns of Thought ... 5

The Process of Thinking 15

Changing Your Course 19

Overcoming Obstacles 25

Mastering Yourself 29

Overcoming Fear 33

The Enemy Of Progress 37

Turning Thoughts Into Reality 45

Resisting Frustration 49

*From the Author of Unexpected Treasures,
Turn on Your Life, and Dream Big Start Small!*

YOU CAN THINK
YOUR WAY TO
SUCCESS

Dr. Mikel Brown

You Can Think Your Way To Success

1208 S Sumac Dr
El Paso, TX 79925

Copyright (c) 2002 by Mikel Brown. All rights reserved
Printed in the United States of America

ISBN: 978-1-930388-37-6

Editorial assistance for CJC Publishing Co. by Charles Babers
Cover design by. CHughes Advertising Agency

All quotations is appropriately noted after the quote

No part of this publication may be reproduced, stored in a retrieval system, or transmitted in any form or by any means, electronic, mechanical, photocopying, recording, scanning, or otherwise, except as permitted under Section 107 or 108 of the 1976 United States Copyright Act, without the prior written permission of the Published. Requests to the Publisher for permission should be addreded to the Permissions Department, CJC Publishing, 1208 Sumac Drive. El Paso, TX 79925, 915-595-137, fax 915-595-1493, or e-mail permcoordinator@cjcpublishing.com.

Limit of Liability/Disclaimer of Warranty: While the publisher and author have used their best efforts in preparing this book, they make no representation or warranties with respect to the accuracy or completeness of the contents of this book and specifically disclaim any implied guarantees. The advice and strategies contained herein may not be suitable for every situation. Neither the publisher nor author shall be liable for any outcome concerning ones finances or business, included but not limited to special, incidental, consequential, or other damages.

CHAPTER ONE

Faith Creates New Incredible Patterns Of Thought

"I believe in Christianity as I believe that the sun has risen: not only because I see it, but because by it I see everything else."

~ C.S. Lewis

CHAPTER ONE

Faith Creates New Incredible Patterns Of Thought

THINKING ONE'S WAY TO SUCCESS IS like planting seeds in the garden of the mind; the more you tend to it with positivity and resilience, the richer the harvest. The most amazing things in life tend to happen right at the moment you're about to give up hope, but your faith in God kicks in and won't allow you to capitulate to the circumstances. At this point, you discover avenues and different ways of doing things you would otherwise have been blind to see.

Faith in God can be a powerful source of motivation, resilience, and hope for many people. Faith can provide a sense of purpose, inspire positive actions, and help people cope with challenges. Every great achievement begins with a thought. Harness the power of your mind, for it is the anvil upon which the sword of success is forged.

Thoughts are the architects of your destiny. The blueprint for success resides in the quality of your thinking. A thought is the spark that ignites the flame of success. You should be compelled to guard and nourish your thought and let it illuminate your path to greatness. As a lighthouse guides ships through the dark, so does positive, faith-thinking guide us through to success. The most potent tool on your journey to success is your mind. Fuel it with positivity, nurture it with knowledge, and steer it with determination. In the symphony of success, thoughts are the first notes.

Your mind is the rudder steering your ship to success, but faith is the powerful engine that drives your life through the rough terrain of the ups and downs of life. Keep it focused, for the voyage to greatness is sailed on the sea of thoughts. Harmonize them well, and you shall create a masterpiece of your life. Here's how faith can make things possible:

It inspires Hope and Optimism: Faith in God can provide a sense of hope and optimism, even in difficult situations. This hope can motivate individuals to keep striving towards their goals, even when they face setbacks. The belief that God, who embodies a power greater than your own, has a plan for people can inspire people to expect good things and to persevere.

Provides Purpose: Faith can provide individuals with a sense of purpose or direction in life. This sense of purpose can drive people to achieve things that they may not have thought possible.

Fosters Resilience: Faith can help individuals to be resilient in the face of adversity. Belief in God's love, care, and guidance can give individuals the strength to overcome challenges, persevere, and stay focused on their goals.

Promotes Positive Behaviors and Attitudes: Many Bible teachings promote virtues such as kindness, patience, humility, and perseverance. These virtues can promote positive behaviors and attitudes that are conducive to success.

Provides a Supportive Community: Religious communities can provide emotional support, practical help, and encouragement. This sense of community can help individuals to stay motivated, to believe in their potential, and to work towards their goals.

Encourages Personal Growth: Many religious beliefs emphasize personal growth, learning, and development. This emphasis can inspire individuals to strive for self-improvement and to seek out opportunities for growth.

Facilitates Coping and Stress Management: Spiritual practices such as prayer, meditation, and attending religious services can help individuals to manage stress, find peace and maintain a positive mindset.

Faith, therefore, can enable a person to believe and achieve incredible things by providing hope, purpose, resilience, and a supportive community. It can promote positive behaviors and attitudes, encourage personal growth, and facilitate coping and stress management. However, it's important to remember that faith is a personal journey, and its impact can vary from person to person. Absolutely, achieving success is often a major goal for many people, and understanding how to do so is crucial.

Keep in mind a few key points when seeking to achieve success. Clearly define what success means to you because everyone's definition of success is different. For some, it might mean financial wealth, for others, it might mean reaching a high level in a career, maintaining good health, or having a happy and healthy family. You must define what success means for you before stretching out to achieve it.

Set Goals, and once you know what success looks like for you, you can start setting short-term and long-term goals. These goals should be S.M.A.R.T. - Specific, Measurable, Achievable, Relevant, and Time-bound. You must create a plan, and after setting your goals, create a detailed plan of how you will achieve them. This might involve furthering your education, seeking mentors, honing your skills, or changing your lifestyle.

Taking action is often mentioned but easily avoided. Take action, your plan is just a dream or a wish until you take action. Start working on your plan and stay consistent. Success often involves a lot of hard work and determination, and it doesn't happen overnight. Perseverance is a key component to achieving success. There will be obstacles and setbacks, but perseverance is key.

Don't let failure discourage you. Instead, use it as a learning experience to improve and push forward. Embrace continuous learning. To be successful, it's important to keep learning and improving. This could be in the form of formal education, professional development, self-study, or experiential learning.

Remember, success is a journey, not a destination. The importance of achieving success varies from person to person. For some, it can bring a sense of accomplishment and validation, for others, it could mean a comfortable lifestyle or personal growth. However, pursuing success should never come at the expense of your health, relationships, or relationship with Christ. It's important to find balance and satisfaction in the journey, as well as, in the achievement of success.

The relationship between success and effort is complex, and their importance can vary based on one's perspective. The Process-Oriented Perspective should never be taken lightly. From this perspective, the effort put into achieving a goal is as important, if not more so, than the outcome itself. This viewpoint emphasizes personal growth, skill development, resilience, and the satisfaction derived from striving toward a goal. It recognizes that success is often a byproduct of hard work and effort. People who adopt this perspective believe in the value of effort as a character and personal development determinant.

The Outcome-Oriented Perspective is from this viewpoint, success is the ultimate measure of value. The focus is on results, achievements, and the tangible outcome of one's work. This perspective tends to be more prevalent in competitive environments or societies where success is often measured by external indicators such as wealth, status, or recognition. In reality, both effort and success are important in their own ways.

The effort is crucial because it fosters growth, resilience, and personal development. We learn, improve and build character through exerting effort and overcoming challenges. Moreover, consistent effort is often a prerequisite for success. On the other hand, success is also important because it provides a sense of achievement, validation and can boost self-esteem. It often brings tangible rewards that can improve one's lifestyle and open new opportunities. However, it's important to remember that success without effort can lead to complacency and lack of fulfillment, while effort without any measure of success can lead to frustration and burnout. Thus, it's crucial to find a balance between the two and to appreciate both the journey (effort) and the destination (success).

Thinking your way to success is a crucial component of achieving your goals. It involves developing a positive mindset, setting clear goals, and adopting effective strategies to reach those goals. With it, you develop a growth mindset. Cultivate a mindset that embraces challenges, is persistent in the face of setbacks, sees the effort as a path to mastery, and learns from criticism. People with a growth mindset believe they can improve their abilities and intelligence through dedication and not just hard work but smart work.

Faith aids your visualization of success. Visualization is a powerful tool. Regularly imagine yourself achieving your goals and experiencing the feelings associated with that success. God gave you an imagination, use it wisely, and don't use it to imagine all the negative things that can occur. That would be a terrible use of the imagination. This can motivate you and make your goals feel more tangible.

Positive affirmations should be orally repeated, not put off using only when you think you need them. Repeat positive statements to yourself that reinforce your belief in God and your ability to achieve your goals. This can help to overwrite negative thought patterns with positive ones. Surround yourself with Godly positive influences. The people you surround yourself with can significantly impact your mindset and outlook.

Seek out individuals who inspire, motivate, and support you, and ignore like the plague, those who are consistently negative and vain seeking. Remember, your income is the average of your ten closest friends.

CHAPTER TWO

The Process of Thinking

"Thinking is the hardest work there is, which is the probable reason why so few engage in it."

~ **Henry Ford**

CHAPTER TWO

The Process of Thinking

SOME PEOPLE BELIEVE THAT THROUGH poverty all lessons of stewardship are learned. I believe that if you are impoverished, you have nothing by which to measure your stewardship. If a person is a fool without money, he will be a fool with money. Having money does not answer questions about your character. In fact, it says very little about who you are. Money is a tool; if you learn to use it wisely, it will never master you. Thinking your way to success starts with changing your view of money. Money is not designed to create fulfillment. If you are convinced that money will solve all of your problems or answer life's questions, you will only discover that a whole new set of problems comes with money. I did not say that having money is a problem. I said that with it comes a whole new set of troubles. Does this mean a person should not have to make money as part of their agenda? No, of course not! However, money should not be the only thing a person uses to measure success. There are myths about money flowing around in the minds of people that are totally outlandish. One of them is that the less money you have the happier you will become, and the more money you have the less happy you will be. I have also heard it the other way around. The more money you have the happier you will become and the less money you have, the more miserable you will be. I cannot discard how having more than enough money can make life's pleasures enjoyable. Neither can I cast off how not having enough money can limit some of the pleasures of life. Do not misunderstand me! Money has its place, but not as a tool to measure a person's character.

CHAPTER THREE

Changing Your Course

"You can change your course if you can define your goals."

~ **Dr. Mikel Brown**

CHAPTER THREE

Changing Your Course

PEOPLE MUST BE ABLE TO DISCERN OR define for themselves what success is. You can change your course if you can define your goals. What matters to you? What is success to you? To have a financial goal is not declaring that money is your only interest. Riches are the most frivolous commodities in the world. I am not interested in money but in the things for which money is merely a symbol. If your ultimate goal is to assist people in qualifying for the purchase of a home, and you are making money because of it, then why not set financial goals to further your passion? On the other hand, if your interest is to make money at the expense of your client, then you need a checkup from the neck up. When money is your ultimate goal, you will lie to your clients just to obtain what you want. With some people, success turns their heads. With others, it is too bad it does not wring their necks.

I have read articles written by counselors and motivational speakers on matters that concern the mind. There are not many who can truly define and intelligently articulate how matters of the heart become habitual unless they have some belief in the supernatural. Not everything can be tied directly to the mind as an end, especially when they believe that our hearts manufacture our thoughts. There are several sources from which we receive stimuli that register in our brains: through the eyes, ears, nose, touch, taste, and dreams (day or night). My purpose is not to sound technical but to be informed. How can thoughts bypass your eyes, ears, nose, touch, taste, and dreams? What are the materials of a thought? What stimulant is used in order to cause a brain to receive messages? All messages must filter through the brain because that is where all dissecting begins. Our brains operate from the information received. They learn behavior patterns from what is heard, seen, and read. It is the best-made computer in the world. For the mind to establish morals, thoughts must be retrieved and believed. Morals are a belief system through which a person adopts certain thought patterns. The brain, in and of itself, only takes in the information, but the inner self, which is a part of every man, chooses to build from the information received a firmly incorporated foundation for life. Consequently, boundaries are set, and rules are established.

How can the mind recollect if there is nothing in it to recall? Now the mind's capability is highly symbolic and visual. It can imagine practically anything. Meaning it can adapt to bring visualizations to various needs. A "need" can spark a part of the brain that can ignite its imaginative skills. The mind has built-in components for creativity and innovation. The mind can spin off from one thought to produce so many other thoughts that derive from the original.
As powerful as thinking is, you wonder why so few engage in it. There must be deliberate and purposeful thinking on behalf of the individual. I recall watching a television sitcom called "Third Rock", which is about aliens from another planet who came to Earth to explore human life. As three aliens were watching

television, the young alien woman said, "This is amazing! I haven't had to think since looking at this box." What does this say about the American public? Our capacity to think and design is atrophied while viewing television. Our future generation is slowly being reduced to a reflection of television sitcoms and movies. There is nothing wrong with being amused, but don't allow entertainment to put your mind in park (idleness).

When a person has a thought, a bit of fire, the first thing that should be done is it should be written on a piece of paper. The more you look at your written thoughts, the more you feast on them. Words are like drops of dew falling upon thoughts to produce thousands or even millions of mental pictures. I am sure you have heard this repeatedly, but there is a rationale behind it. By writing your thoughts down on paper, you are employing your eyes. When you read your written thoughts aloud, you are engaging your ears and mouth. Suddenly, your thoughts explode into a mushroom of images. These images are simply pictures of success and accomplishment. Once this is locked into your memory bank, your inner man has a clear, focused picture to target. The target is hit when the person's thoughts are converted into passion. If your mind or thinking patterns are invaded by a thought contrary to what you now believe, your mind will quickly dismiss the invading thought.

CHAPTER FOUR

Overcoming Obstacles

"When you can think your way beyond the obvious, nothing can hinder you from succeeding."

~ **Dr. Mikel Brown**

CHAPTER FOUR

Overcoming Obstacles

SUCCESS IS NOT AS DIFFICULT TO ACHIEVE as most people believe. Defining what success is for you may be the most challenging part of all. However, if you can define it, then your success is at the threshold. Spending time to think of what you want and how you plan to achieve it is denotative of where you are going. Nothing can hinder you from succeeding when you can think beyond the obvious.

When Evander Holyfield and Mike Tyson stepped into the ring to fight for the first time, the odds were 9 to 2 in favor of Mike Tyson. I am not a betting man, but my money would have been on the thinker if I were. Mike Tyson would win fights by intimidating his opponents. Holyfield was not the kind of man who was easily alarmed. Holyfield never fought with just brute strength but with his head. A person who can ignore the obvious is a person who can win the heavyweight championship of the world. You may be in a position where the odds are 10 to 1 in favor of your opponent. You are trying to motivate yourself subliminally, but your opponent seems overwhelming. This is when you must dismiss the obvious and believe you can conquer them. If you refuse to think you can, you will run away and wonder what could have happened.

Obstacles are an inevitable part of our life's journey. They challenge our mettle and, if approached correctly, can propel us to new heights of personal and professional growth. The most dynamic way to overcome these challenges lies in cultivating a mindset of adaptability.

Adaptability is the ability to adjust oneself promptly and efficiently in response to changing circumstances. It signifies an open mindset, flexibility, and the readiness to innovate, which are crucial in navigating obstacles. Consider obstacles as detours rather than roadblocks. Each obstacle presents an opportunity to learn, grow, and recalibrate our strategies. A dynamic approach requires us to continuously assess our situation, gather information, and explore various solutions instead of adhering rigidly to one plan. However, adaptability should not be confused with aimlessness. It's about flexibility in methods, not goals. A clear vision of the desired outcome gives adaptability a direction and purpose.

Incorporating resilience alongside adaptability further bolsters this dynamic approach. Resilience aids in maintaining positivity and perseverance in the face of adversity, reinforcing the adaptive process. To conclude, overcoming obstacles is less about the force applied and more about the adaptability and resilience adopted. Embracing adaptability allows us to transform obstacles into opportunities, fostering an ongoing learning, growth, and success cycle.

CHAPTER FIVE

Mastering Yourself

"You will never master what you allow to enslave you."

~ **Dr. Mikel Brown**

CHAPTER FIVE

Mastering Yourself

IT WAS OBVIOUS, THAT IN COMPARISON, young David of the Bible was smaller than Goliath the giant. David thought past the giant's stature and became so consumed with the thought that he could defeat the giant that he ran towards him and threw a rock. It was not the rock killing the giant that brought David instant fame and respect; it was his courage and uncommon way of accepting adulation. Decapitating the giant showed how David was someone who knew how to "get ahead" in life. (Laugh) David saw what he had done as nothing more than what anyone else could have done. Despite his lack of experience in adult matters, he stood head and shoulders above all the others.

You will never conquer the things to which you surrender. You will never master what you allow to enslave you. If fear keeps you from starting a business, then fear is all that will be needed to keep you from moving forward. You will never take the first step in changing your life because your life is controlled by fear. Fear will paralyze anyone who will submit to its mental slavery, which is when a person surrenders to another the power to control their mind. If a man is in prison, the bars that circumscribe his life do not necessarily enslave him. The bars may enclose your body, but not your mind. If you have failed in a particular area of life, it does not give failure the right to control your destiny. Success is not final, and failure is not fatal.

How can a person think of sentencing their whole life to failure because of one mistake? This is similar to throwing out a basket of apples because of one bad apple. If a part of your life is not quite the way you planned, you still have much life left. Change your thinking pattern when it comes to disappointments and frustrations. This is no reason to place yourself in the hands of the undertaker. Life is full of twists and turns, stoppages and delays, successes and accomplishments. I have learned to expect certain things in life. There can be no success without struggle. When pregnant with a vision or a dream, opposition will come while you are pushing to deliver. Resistance is a part of life. This planet does not freely surrender its resources, you must hammer, drill, dig, or dynamite out of it what you want. It is there for anyone who dares to take it. If you want something out of life, don't ask someone else whether or not you can have it.

CHAPTER SIX

Overcoming Fear

"One of your greatest surprises will be when you discover that you can do what you were always afraid to do."

~ **Dr. Mikel Brown**

CHAPTER SIX

Overcoming Fear

YOU MUST CHOOSE TO IMAGINE THE unimaginable, to believe the unbelievable, and to think the unthinkable. Therefore, the unimaginable will be imagined, the unbelievable will be believed, and the unthinkable will be thought, and nothing will keep you from succeeding. Dare to imagine what others call preposterous, believe what others say cannot be accomplished, and think of what others are too afraid to ponder.

Fear is a primal human emotion that signals danger and, in some cases, acts as a protective mechanism. However, when fear becomes paralyzing, it morphs into an overwhelming force that prevents individuals from conquering obstacles and attaining personal success. In these cases, fear stops being a protector and transforms into a captor.

Paralyzing fear is more than just a fleeting sensation of discomfort; it's a debilitating state that clouds judgment, obscures potential, and fosters a cycle of self-doubt and inaction. Its roots may lie in past failures, fear of the unknown, or a perceived lack of skills or resources. Regardless of its source, paralyzing fear keeps individuals stuck in a zone of perpetual inertia, halting progress and stymieing personal and professional growth.

It's essential to understand that paralyzing fear is not an insurmountable obstacle. While it may seem impenetrable, there exist various strategies for its dissolution. Firstly, acknowledging the existence of fear is pivotal. Denying or avoiding the emotion only allows it to fester and amplify. This recognition serves as a springboard toward understanding the underlying causes of this fear.

Analyzing fear by identifying specific triggers can empower individuals to anticipate and plan for these instances. In this step, fear can be reframed from being a barrier to a stepping stone toward growth. Acknowledging that failure isn't a sign of inadequacy, but a natural part of life's learning curve, can help assuage these fears. Certain techniques, such as breathing steadily, can foster a sense of calm, enabling individuals to handle fear-inducing situations better.

In conclusion, while paralyzing fear can seem overwhelming, it is not an insurmountable hurdle. Individuals can conquer their fears through self-recognition, reframing mindset, utilizing relaxation techniques, and seeking professional help when necessary. As a result, they can transform these fears from barriers into bridges toward personal success. Overcoming fear is not just about dispelling negative emotions but also reclaiming one's path to self-fulfillment and achievement.

One of your greatest surprises will be when you discover you can do what you were always afraid to do. The only thing keeping you from doing it is not doing it. Do you realize what an awesome creation you are, that absolutely nothing refrains from you that you can imagine doing? The capacity to succeed in anything you can imagine is possible.

CHAPTER SEVEN

The Enemy of Progress

*"If a friend does not respect your dreams, he is
an enemy of your progress."*

~ **Dr. Mikel Brown**

CHAPTER SEVEN

The Enemy of Progress

I F YOU LIVE ANY AMOUNT OF TIME ON THIS earth, you will discover that life will give you absolutely nothing you deserve but everything you work to get. I refuse to leave my life to chance or fate. I take life very seriously! I only have one shot at fulfilling it, so I cannot leave it in the hands of someone who will limit or demean it. If you gain a perspective on life based on what someone else thinks of you, you will be limited by his or her thoughts. Most people will only tell you what you cannot do to limit what you can achieve. They will laugh at your dreams and goals because they do not respect your abilities.

If a friend does not respect your dreams, he is an

enemy of your progress. These are the kinds of friends you do not need. They will sentence you to failure and kick you for failing. It can be a brother, a childhood friend, a cousin, or even a parent. Some of them mean no harm, it is just the way they are.

Changing your thinking patterns requires tremendous diligence. Nothing changes without making an assertive effort. Of course, if the majority of the population finds it too difficult to go against the flow, anyone who swims upstream will face opposition from those going downstream. As you think your way to success, some will attempt to change the direction of your life through suggestions and questions. Most people have a trail of unfinished tasks due to pressures or difficulties. Because many people do not accomplish what they set out to do, they will give you every reason why you cannot succeed at your goals. When you stop working on your dreams, it is because you have thoughts of obstacles that intimidate you. Change the thoughts of intimidation into thoughts of strength and press through. When you begin to think that what you are attempting to do is more difficult than expected, nullify the difficulties by working harder. You will discover that your success will be sweeter.

"Wise men are instructed by reason; men of less understanding, by experience; the most ignorant, by necessity; the beasts by nature," said Marcus Tullius Cicero, a Roman orator and statesman. Wisdom is a word used to describe the great minds of yesterday and today that appears to be losing their celebrity status. Could it be that focusing on one's thoughts is outdated? With education on a decline and the dummying down of textbooks in the public school system, it is no wonder why so many people cannot think their way out of a plastic bag. Today's youth are not challenged to stretch their brains, broaden their horizons and grasp their visions. Calculators are used in math classes, and multiple-choice questions are provided on tests instead of essays. These make it easier for the students so that they can pass to the next grade. How can you graduate from high school reading on an eighth-grade level? Is it fair to expect out of the next generation what we have not prepared them to undertake?

Seven out of ten college students confessed to cheating on an exam. Instead of thinking your way to success, some people are convinced you can cheat your way to success. I know a businessman with a Master's Degree in Marketing who claimed he cheated throughout his undergraduate and graduate years. To say the least, this man has no integrity at all. Although he does well in business, he continues to get into financial problems because he does not have basic managerial skills to keep a business running efficiently. All the new technology we have today seems to be robbing humanity of the greatest ability given...the power to think. Why think when we have computers to think for us, one might say. If society continues in the direction it is going, we will have a bunch of misfits by the year 2050.

Please, do not take out of context what I am saying. I agree wholeheartedly with technology. I strongly believe in the human race. We can invent computers to do many things, but it is a poor substitute for a brain. It is a medical fact that if we do not use our brain, it will start to degenerate. The brain is a muscle that must be exercised in order to keep it vibrant and energetic.

Thinking, thinking, thinking! No one ever succeeded in something without first giving serious thought to it. Your mornings would change if you transformed the way you thought of them. The same is true of your financial status, family life, job, business, and your golf game. You really can think your way to success. It may sound like an infomercial, but it is true. What would you say about people who strongly think and believe that they can do what they have never seen done before? Certainly, you can think of a few people that already meet this qualification. Would you like to place yourself on this list of doers?

I have several true stories that will absolutely blow your mind. A few years ago I had an associate who was constantly trying to get me to ski to the snowy New Mexico mountains. I had never gone skiing before in my life and for me to attend this event meant one thing; if I went, I would have to picture myself skiing. I told my friend I could ski, even though I had never done it before. The look on his face suggested that I was a total idiot. He had been skiing for years and was very efficient at the sport. He could not understand how I could make such a statement without prior experience. Most people need the experience to attempt to accomplish something. I need only a mental picture of what I can do.

CHAPTER EIGHT

Turning Thoughts Into Reality

"All of your failures and accomplishments are reviewed in the mind before they go onto the production line. You can never do what you can never imagine."

~ **Dr. Mikel Brown**

CHAPTER EIGHT

Turning Thoughts Into Reality

I WAS VISITING THE STATE OF CALIFORNIA when an associate of mine asked if I would like to go ice skating. I had never gone ice skating before in my life but could always see myself ice skating. When we arrived at the skating rink, I thought, "How can I stand and balance myself on such a thin blade?" It was easy! When my associate got on the ice, he was showing off his skills. I am certain that he assumed that I would be holding on to the rail because I had never ice skated in my life. Ha, ha! The laugh was on him. I started ice skating backward and then turned around. He could not believe it. He thought I had lied to him about never ice skating and could not convince him otherwise.

In my mind, I had ice-skated a thousand times, but physically I had never ice-skated before. I live by the philosophy that I can achieve anything if I see myself accomplishing it. The key to all that you would like to achieve in life is not in the hands of someone else but in your own. You possess the power and the ability to do anything. God created you with the most awesome tool given to mankind, the ability to think. All of your failures and accomplishments are reviewed in the mind before they go onto the production line. You can never do what you can never imagine!

It cannot be an accident if you would like to experience a prolific life. A productive life must be deliberate. If your desire for something persists, it could very well mean that you are hungry enough for it to pursue it with all of your heart. People who are unwilling to lose in life rarely do.

One of your greatest thrills in engaging your mind will be when you make up your mind to do something. Your goals will be accomplished in just a matter of time. Listen! You owe it to yourself, your family, and others to succeed. Life is the single greatest opportunity extended to you. It remains your choice to change your thinking from "I can't" to "I know I can! I know I can! Moreover, believe me, you will. Striving for perfection is self-defeating; striving to become better takes you one step further up the ladder of development.

There was a sitcom that came on television weekly that I remember only vaguely, but I do recall the ending of the theme song. It stands out in my mind like a beacon of light. The show was the Mary Tyler Moore Show. I don't know why I admired this theme song so much. It reminded me of a person fighting against all odds to succeed. To this very day, I still sing the ending of this song. "You're gonna to make it after all..." were the ending words to this song. I know this can sound a bit sentimental and even comical, but I assure you that neither is the case. When you are trying to find your way through the labyrinth of life and locating an exit seems virtually impossible, you will take hold of anything that will provide hope. I locked onto these words like my life depended on them. To some extent, this is the theme song of my life.

CHAPTER NINE

Resisting Frustration

"Frustration does not dictate failure, it simply points to the fact that you are in the process of finding another way to achieve your objective."

~ **Dr. Mikel Brown**

CHAPTER NINE

Resisting Frustration

YOU MIGHT BE THAT PERSON WHO has tried seemingly everything but to no avail. I know how it feels not to want to hear another motivational tape, see another infomercial on starting a business, or attend another seminar on how to be successful. You just want to relegate your life to a nine-to-five job and somehow find contentment. Yet there is a burning desire in you to do better. Allow me to make a few suggestions. Success is not what you do but who you are. Frustrations will come because you are making attempts to better your life and the lives of your family. Everyone has a rage that will surface when they are doing something and it does not turn out the way they thought it would. Frustration does not dictate failure; it simply points to the fact that you are in the process of finding another way to achieve your objective. It is a God-given emotion to signal to you to try another way. If you are frustrated sometimes, it means you are doing something. It's the person who never feels the rage of frustration that might actually signal being complacent.

Complacency is a detriment to your progress. It suggests that the complacent person is satisfied with his or her present condition and will avoid all challenges that disrupt his or her apathy. You are on the right track when you feel disappointed. It is designed to push you, not recline you.

Pursuit is the design for life. What I mean by this is that although life is given, the treasures of life must be taken. You are supposed to be the predator in life, not the prey. This earthly life is not designed to hand you preferential treatment. It will turn over its rewards to those who persevere to the end of their pursuit.

One evening in my yard, my son and I were playing baseball. He wanted me to do all the pitching while he did all the hitting. After swinging consecutive times and missing the ball, he became angry and frustrated and wanted me to pitch to him underhandedly. Although he was only six, he was at a point when lessons needed to be taught and exemplified. Needless to say, I refused to placate his desire for ease to satisfy his lack of diligence. I told him, "Son if you keep swinging, you will eventually hit the ball." Once he accepted that I wouldn't make it easy for him, he continued to adjust until he consistently hit the ball over my head. If you could have seen the look on his face, you would have celebrated him because of his accomplishments. My son expressed such a hunger to play that he was willing to do what was uncomfortable for him. When your mental picture changes in the area of defeat, your defeats will become no more.

Life is not going to deviate from its design for you because you find it difficult, but it will surrender to you when you defeat its challenges.

About The Author

DR. MIKEL BROWN is an author, businessperson, restaurateur, and religious leader who resides in El Paso, Texas. He is a Licensed Professional Counselor with more than 40 years of experience. He has helped many people achieve success in business, marriage, personal development and peak performance.

Dr. Brown has helped people from rocky marriages to rocketing careers. His private client protégés list range from active and retired professional sports personalities to more than a hundred small business owners. He has over 14 books published, such as *When Lambs Turns Into Lions, Dream Big Start Small, Turn on Your Life, Unexpected Treasures, How to Fix Your Marriage without Using a Hammer,* and *Building Wealth from the Ground Up.*

THE POCKET MOTIVATOR BOOK SERIES

DR. MIKEL A. BROWN

Now You Can Take The Wisdom of Dr. Brown With You Wherever You Go!

GET YOUR COPIES
TODAY!

www.MikelBrown.com

www.ingramcontent.com/pod-product-compliance
Lightning Source LLC
Chambersburg PA
CBHW061805070526
44586CB00023B/2724